JOHN TRESSEL

AFTER ARMAGEDDON

HOW TO CONQUER YOUR DOOMSDAY FEARS

ENCOURAGE
PUBLISHING
NEW ALBANY, INDIANA

© John Tressel, 2022

All rights reserved. Written permission must be secured from the publisher to use or reproduce any part of this book, except for brief quotations in reviews, endorsements, or articles.

Published and printed in the United States of America, for worldwide distribution.

Library of Congress Control Number: 2022938530
ISBN: 978-1-7343231-3-9

Cataloguing data:
Tressel, John
After Armageddon: How to Conquer Your Doomsday Fears
1. Oral communication-Religious aspects- Christianity
2. The Christian Life (Religion—Philosophy)
3. Christian Living—Spiritual growth

Dewey Decimal Classification: 248: Christian experience, practice, life

Cover and interior design by Jonathan Lewis
Edited by Leslie Turner

All Scripture quotations are taken from the New King James Version®. Copyright © 1982 by Thomas Nelson. Used by permission. All rights reserved.

Published by: Encourage Publishing, New Albany, Indiana, USA - www.encouragepublishing.com

CONTENTS

INTRODUCTION	*1*
PART I A Roadmap To Armageddon	*5*
CHAPTER 1 World Events, War, and the Media	*12*
CHAPTER 2 Man-Made Disasters and Prophecy	*20*
CHAPTER 3 Natural Disasters and Prophecy	*33*
CHAPTER 4 The Trail of the Antichrist	*42*
CHAPTER 5 Birth Pangs of a New World	*50*
PART II Armageddon and the Church	*63*
CHAPTER 6 The Church Defined	*65*
CHAPTER 7 The Church in the End Times	*74*
CHAPTER 8 The Jewish Reconciliation	*86*
CHAPTER 9 God Works in the Unified Church	*97*

PART III After Armageddon   *107*
CHAPTER 10 Facing Armageddon   *110*
ABOUT THE AUTHOR   *124*
ENDNOTES   *126*

INTRODUCTION

So, here we are together for a few moments. Neither one of us ever expected to meet under such conditions. Discussing the **end of the world** seems to be a rather intense question—the type of discussion usually reserved for the experts that we never get to meet face to face. But you have decided to investigate the subject yourself. You want to know what is going on in this topsy-turvy world.

I am glad to meet you, and I would like to invite you into my life to accompany me on this winding road. Right now, at the beginning of this curious voyage, I would like you to understand my motivations.

I am a pastor and conference speaker. My wife and I are American and have been preaching the Gospel in France since 1976. We have been fortunate and blessed to be able to work among evangelicals, Protestants, and, at times, Catholics. We have also worked in many different countries in Europe and beyond. This experience has allowed us to see the Lord move not only in Europe but also globally.

You, on the other hand, have questions in your heart about what to expect. You have probably heard multiple theories concerning the end of the world. In fact, it is highly unlikely that you have *never* heard an "end of the world" storyline in media or entertainment. The media surrounds us with this type of speculative news because it sells! For example, several movies and well over one hundred books are in print concerning the false Mayan 2012 "end of the world" theory. Those questions in your heart are put there by God himself and are very valid:

> *He has made everything beautiful in its time. Also, He has put eternity in their hearts, except that no one can find out the work that God does from beginning to end.*
> —Ecclesiastes 3:11

The Bible tells us often that no one will know exactly how or what God is doing and what will happen. If anyone claims to know, watch out! Still, there is much we can learn from the Bible about the end of the world, including how to rise above any fear we may have about it. In this book, there is no mysticism, no coded enigmas. The focus is on the simple words of Jesus and certain prophets who have been speaking to us since antiquity. Now is the moment to better understand the times we live in; know that the Lord will accompany us on this journey of understanding—all the way.

Can I make a small request before we start? If you are angry with the Church for any reason, **would you forgive the Church for her many, many errors?** Many people who are on bad terms with God are, in fact, angry with the Church. Again, please forgive us. I could elaborate on all the wrong the Church has done, but that could take up too many precious lines. Hear my heart; please forgive the Church! Doing so will free your heart from that burden, and free your mind to consider openly what the Bible says about Armageddon. Otherwise you may miss it entirely!

Let us begin our curious voyage.

PART I

A ROADMAP TO ARMAGEDDON

A good map and a few road signs can guide you along the road we are about to travel together. You need to know what to expect. Perhaps you won't like all the road signs as they pop up, but you'll decide that yourself. Whatever your decision, that is great! I will be upfront with you as to what to expect and, if you choose to go your own way, we can separate and stay friends.

Before we all had GPS on our phones, people used road maps to find their way. Learning to read a road map can be challenging without a key! Below are six keys to following the road map of *After Armageddon*—a few assumptions on which this book is based:

1. The Bible addresses the subject accurately, and the Bible's words on the subject are not merely symbolic.

This book is based on the belief that the Bible is the Word of God. Everybody has an opinion concerning religion and holy books, even if they don't believe in God or religion. I want to present you with my conceptual framework of the world's end based on the Bible, without attacking other belief structures.

In the larger circle of Christianity, there are two different opinions concerning the end of the world. Some believe that the prophetic words in the Bible are merely examples, perhaps metaphors or something that is purely symbolic. I do not subscribe to that idea.

Here is an excellent example: Jesus spoke of earthquakes in Matthew 24 as a sign preceding his return. It seems reasonable to believe that he was speaking of actual earthquakes. Could it be at all reasonable to think that he was talking of anything else but real **earthquakes**? I submit this to your judgment. Yes, interpreting every word of the Bible literally can also do a disservice to reasoning minds. Trying to walk such a tight interpretive rope is an acrobatic feat!

Balanced biblical interpretation leads us to first acknowledge what is evident in the text before any in-depth examination. To put it another way, before you start reading between the lines, try reading what is *on* the lines.

2. Simplicity is the key to understanding what the Bible says about this theme.

Wise men from ancient times until now have sought to understand what the end of the world entails. Many theories have come and gone. But now, it feels as if the end of the world is all happening before our eyes. Or is it? The answer is: it's complicated.

Complexity and simplicity are not brothers. Complexity often happens when people project their interpretations onto Bible text.

I wanted to avoid writing the following thought, but I cannot betray my own heart. People who believe in their own superior intelligence often try to convince us of their intelligence through complex theories, vivid speculation, and lofty, condescending language—the tools of their trade. Is it possible to avoid this trap? Let us try together.

For example, there are many hard sayings in the book of Daniel in the Old Testament. It is one of the weightier prophetic books of the Bible. Daniel gave us numerous prophecies that speak of the rise and fall of the world's kingdoms. His prophetic words are extraordinarily accurate. You can read about their fulfillment in any ancient world history book. By the inspiration of the Holy Spirit, Daniel wrote world history before it happened. Did you know this amazing fact?

But in this same book, you can find that some of Daniel's sayings defy the most probing human investigation. We just don't know what all his prophetic proclamations mean, so why should we try to understand things that remain unexplainable for the time being? Forcing an interpretation of prophetic **hard sayings** is not profitable for either of us.

3. We will concentrate on what we can understand.

Here, you will not find complicated theories of secret political, spiritual, mystical, or economic plots: no secret codes and the like you may have read about or seen in movies. While conspiracy theories may have some truth, they usually add more bulk on the fantastic side than on the practical, provable side. A monumental task of this book is avoiding unfounded speculation. It is a fact that Jesus and most of the New Testament authors developed prophetic themes. Let us dwell on what Jesus and the apostles said.

This subject is so vast that it is challenging to cover the topic adequately. I will discuss the main Bible themes on the subject. You are invited to read along, and then make your conclusions.

A note: It is impossible to eradicate my personal beliefs from the text. On rare occasions, I will present you with a point of view that is purely my opinion. At that point, I will label the content as a **theory.**

4. This information is not specific to any church, denomination, cult, or sect.

There is a significant difference between this presentation and those of various cults and/or sects who often sell their organization through their unique interpretation of the Bible and a very distinctive "end of the world" plan. You could not come to their conclusions by reading the Bible alone. Almost all have added what they refer to as "sacred texts" to the Bible. *After Armageddon* talks about the end of the world through a biblical lens only—no added text.

5. We will talk about fear—and hope.

Apocalyptic fear drives much of the media's presentation concerning the end of the world.

Horror films and end-time plots are massive revenue sources from Bollywood to Hollywood (more on this in Chapter One). Virtually all the movies concerning the end of the world are saturated with despair. There is no hope because the world as we know it will **end** in these movies with a **bang**, and then it is **finished**—there *is* no "after" Armageddon—a very brutal ending indeed! There are few exceptions to this scenario: the world ends, we fall off the edge, and that is all she wrote. **This book will give you hope.**

Most people are afraid of the direction the world is taking. How about you? Are you afraid of all the change you see coming? If that is your case, I assure you that fear is normal! We don't ordinarily appreciate an adventurous trip into uncharted and dangerous territory, but let's be honest; it looks as if **the world is at the brink of significant change—a tipping point.** Nobody in the marketplace dares to pretend that we are about to enter a period of long-term stability, world peace, or economic prosperity; **nobody**, except a few metaphysical trekkers.

A discussion concerning the **fear** of the end of the world is not very comfortable or reassuring. But this reality is before us and has now become entrenched in our society. A Serbian record label even released a record in 2011 called *Apocalyptic Fear*. Let us deal with these fears together and listen to what the Bible and Jesus might have to say.

6. This book may not answer all of your questions.

You will find potholes in the road we are about to travel. Let us try to avoid them, but you still need to know they are there. Things you don't understand or agree with create potholes. Don't be surprised by them. You may be seeking an answer to a specific question, but you don't find it. Perhaps the treatment of a subject doesn't agree with you. But, just because there is a pothole in the road doesn't mean that you shouldn't keep on driving For now, steer around it and read further.

OK, you now have the road map for this book. Start your motor, put your car in gear, and let us move on down the road.

CHAPTER 1

WORLD EVENTS, WAR, AND THE MEDIA

Does everyone believe that our world will come to an end? The things Jesus said about the signs of the end of the world are so numerous that it is impossible to ignore them. You can spot them through a casual reading of the four gospels in the New Testament: Matthew, Mark, Luke, and John. You can observe the signs daily in the news about world events. Almost all of the sixty-six books of the Bible describe that **terrible** and **glorious** day. Sometimes, these concepts aren't easy to understand because they are often poetic or shrouded in mystical imagery. The verses proposed in this chapter should be easy to grasp.

For those who have the heart of an adventurer, a visit to your local bookstore will reveal a vast number of book titles covering the **apocalypse**. That is the generally accepted word describing the end of the world, interchangeable with the word, "Armageddon."

At one time, I counted the number of film themes that focused on the end of the world. Several years ago, I stopped counting. There were too many. Not to be left behind, Netflix and other Internet streaming services have followed suit. The stories are often spectacular. The media industry is not ashamed of the money spent on fantasized plots and extravagant special effects. The themes vary widely, and numerous works refer to the Bible, either directly or indirectly!

Where do we start our exploration of the end of the world? Generally, people recognize the Bible as the most exact and reliable prophetic document of all time. The remarkable precision, proven through historical fulfillment, is there for all to verify. Compare this to the occult visions of Nostradamus. Some of his predictions have come to pass, but, his prophecies are usually vague, inexact, and an extravagant embellishment of the future. His works make for exciting reading, but his track record is not brilliant.

So, what did Jesus say about the end of the world? He made references throughout the gospels, but one chapter has a condensed version of his future vision. The place to find much of today's and tomorrow's news is Matthew 24. There are also parallels in Mark 13 and Luke 21. I will include passages here for your convenience, but if you have a Bible, find these books at the beginning of the New Testament and read for yourself.

> *And you will hear of wars and rumors of wars. See that you are not troubled; for all these things must come to pass, but the end is not yet. For nation will rise against nation, and kingdom against kingdom.*
>
> —Matthew 24:6–7a

My father served in World War I. The destruction of human life and the infrastructure in Europe are something we cannot imagine. My father was so affected by the war that he could not begin to explain what he had experienced. Today, only a few remain who saw the destruction of World War II. Since then, regional wars have come and gone. The actual situation leads us to some observations:

1. News networks have increased their "bad news" broadcasts. We are instantly aware of conflicts all over the world. Over time, this wears out the human heart. Do this test if you follow the daily news: Does a day pass without hearing of an armed conflict? I would simply ask you to be aware of the level of tension throughout the world.

Of course, wars have always vexed our human tribe. Always! Our twenty-first century environment has significantly changed, and Jesus nailed it: "***You will hear of wars and rumors of wars.***" The rumor machine came up to speed with the war in Vietnam. I was in the United States, watching the conflicts as they played out daily. In the history of our planet, almost instant news coverage had never happened before! Today, we hear regular reports of terrorism, countries building up armaments and testing missiles. I think you recognize that "wars and rumors of wars" have significantly added to our daily stress.

2. War death counts have actually decreased, according to the Global Change Data Lab in a report based on data through 2020. Their researchers wrote, "The absolute number of war deaths has been declining since 1946. In some years in the early post-war era, around half a million people died through direct violence in wars, in contrast, in 2016, the number of all battle-related deaths in conflicts involving at least one [country] was 87,432."[1]

The Peace Research Institute Oslo (PRIO) produced a white paper in 2018 entitled, "Trends in Armed Conflict, 1946-2017." They concluded the following: "Since the end of the Cold War, the armed conflict trend has [gone] generally downward… This does not, however, suggest that the threat of conflict is likely to disappear any time soon, especially given the rise in non-state conflicts and the growth of the Islamic State."[2]

The point here is that the tension, real or anticipated, adds to our fears about Armageddon. Always boiling under the surface is the **horrific potential** for armed conflict. Get out your history books: we went from stones to swords; from swords to cannonballs and rifles; from cannonballs and rifles to bombs: from there, we went to giant bombs with aircraft and missile delivery systems. We kept going with atomic bombs and sophisticated war machines. We have yet to see their full potential developed. We have no idea what the addition of Artificial Intelligence to the equation could mean.

Today, what is the potential of world destruction? Here is all the **doom and gloom** that you may have expected.

The Doomsday Clock. A band of scientists speaks to this moment in history by developing a "clock" that places the apocalypse at midnight and uses the threat of nuclear annihilation—the greatest threat to humanity and the planet—as the minute hand of the clock. "The Bulletin of the Atomic Scientists," founded in 1945 by some of those who were involved in developing the first atomic weapon through the Manhattan Project, says this:

"The decision to move (or to leave in place) the minute hand of the Doomsday Clock is made every year by the Bulletin's Science and Security Board in consultation with its Board of Sponsors, [including] 13 Nobel laureates. The Clock has become a universally recognized indicator of the world's vulnerability to catastrophe from nuclear weapons, climate change, and disruptive technologies in other domains."[3]

At its inception, the clock was set at 11:53 p.m. Every year the minute hand is moved forward or backward, depending on the current global situation. In January 2020, the clock ticked forward to 100 seconds to midnight.[4]

That ominous imagery might cause us to reflect on what the apostle Peter said:

> *But the day of the Lord will come as a thief in the night, in which the heavens will pass away with a great noise, and the elements will melt with fervent heat; both the earth and the works that are in it will be burned up.*
>
> —2 Peter 3:10

This scripture relates current events through a biblical explanation of the end times. The Bible and the evening news are telling us the same story!

As the final editing of this book is in process, Russia's invasion of Ukraine entered its tenth week. Speculations are flying like dandelion seeds in the wind. The Doomsday Clock remains at 100 seconds to midnight as of spring 2022, in spite of the world's fear the war could lead to use of weapons of mass destruction. Horrific death counts on the news every night, each lost life a tragedy, are still far from reaching the loss of life experienced in World War II.

However, the consequences of this war affect the entire world. Before the invasion, Ukraine provided 8% to 13% of key grains to the world supply, and 47% of the world's sunflower oil.[5] Cyber-attacks threaten business and finance systems, ocean tankers are being held up or delayed worldwide, supply chains once again are interrupted, fear is seizing people's hearts, and the economies of many nations are suffering.

[**Theory**: *This invasion interrupted a decades-long period of peace in Europe. In this broken situation, new violence will escalate in other unsuspecting parts of the world. This aggression will enflame the hearts of evil people elsewhere, and embolden them to do likewise.*]

For the next four chapters we will connect more world events to scripture; after all, it is these very events that probably drew you to read this book. However, as you read and learn about these connections, let me encourage you to keep reading! I promised you a way to overcome your doomsday fears, and that path is up ahead!

CHAPTER 2

MAN-MADE DISASTERS AND PROPHECY

Let's take a look first at worldwide disasters that were brought on by man himself.

FOOD SUPPLY

> "For nation will rise against nation, and kingdom against kingdom. And there will be famines, pestilences, and earthquakes in various places."
>
> —Matthew 24:7

Here are some corresponding verses that come from the last book of the Bible.

> *And I heard a voice in the midst of the four living creatures saying, "A quart of wheat for a denarius, and three quarts of*

barley for a denarius; and do not harm the oil and the wine."

When He opened the fourth seal, I heard the voice of the fourth living creature saying, "Come and see." So I looked, and behold, a pale horse. And the name of him who sat on it was Death, and Hades followed with him. And power was given to them over a fourth of the earth, to kill with sword, with hunger, with death, and by the beasts of the earth.

—Revelation 6:6-8

The United Nations monitors world hunger and reports on the situation regularly on their website, where this quote was found:

"The global hunger crisis caused by conflict—and now compounded by COVID-19—is moving into a dangerous phase, the head of the UN World Food Program (WFP) said on Thursday [September 2020], stressing stressed that, without resources, a wave of famine could sweep the globe, overwhelming nations already weakened by years of instability."[6]

Numerous links exist in the food chain, from food production to becoming a meal on our dinner table. Many people believe that we can feed the planet. That is possible! Each indicator of general world stability contributes, in some way, to our capacity to provide food for the earth. When a specific link weakens, the food supply diminishes.

Food supply is like a car engine. It's great when all the parts are working well. But watch out when the car parts start breaking. This is something many of us have experienced first-hand. Many countries, including the United States, have experienced severe supply chain interruptions throughout the coronavirus pandemic, causing empty grocery store shelves and panic buying. In less affluent countries, the effects are much more severe. Many other supplies have been interrupted as well, including medicines and equipment parts to keep our lives running. Food and water shortages, however, affect everyone.

Here is a checklist of the potential threats to the food distribution supply chain. Supply chains are directly affected by societal troubles.
Our food supply depends on the strength of all the links in the chain.

Pandemics	Partially paralyze food supplies
Armed conflicts	Destroy agricultural land and food distribution

Financial crisis	Makes food more expensive
Natural disasters	Hinder production and block effective distribution
Man-made disasters (including global warming and pollution)	Destroy or reduce food supply and agricultural land
Electrical failure	Stops heat, refrigeration, food preparation, and light
Governmental instability	Leads to corruption and negatively affects distribution

FINANCE

James, the brother of Jesus, brings money into the equation of the last days as he describes the collapse of the world economy.

Come now, you rich, weep and howl for your miseries that are coming upon you! Your riches are corrupted, and your garments are moth-eaten. Your gold and silver are corroded, and their corrosion will be a witness against you and will eat your flesh like fire. You have heaped up treasure in the last days.

—James 5:1-3

Many of the world's governments have gone into deep debt to keep their people as comfortable as possible during the pandemic, often when their national economies were already in trouble. This may turn out to be an even a bigger problem than the coronavirus. Many economists draw our attention to the folly of rising national debt. When an economy is not sustainable, the consequences will show up sooner or later. Individuals as well as nations will find themselves in precarious positions because they were not prepared for the economic disaster.

[**Theory**: *Because of COVID many people have gone through financial tragedy. But that will be eclipsed by what nations will go through. We haven't yet seen the worst.*]

The Bible tells us our economic woes will get worse—much worse:

> *"They will throw their silver into the streets, and their gold will be like refuse;*
>
> *Their silver and their gold will not be able to deliver them in the day of the wrath of the Lord;"*

—Ezekiel 7:19a

But what about the condition of mankind itself?

WICKEDNESS

> *"And because lawlessness will abound, the love of many will grow cold."*
> —Matthew 24:12

I have a friend named Gary who regularly told me that he preferred cats to humans. I'd push him a bit. "Gary, how can this be?" He was deeply hurt by family, friends, and casual acquaintances. He became allergic to his fellow kind. Like Gary, humanity is hurting. Most of that pain is not caused by air pollution, but it comes from our own race. We pass many on the streets every day that are in relational collapse.

The apostle Paul steps in here to explain the condition of the human heart at the end of days:

> *But know this, that in the last days perilous times will come: For men will be lovers of themselves, lovers of money, boasters, proud, blasphemers, disobedient to parents, unthankful, unholy, unloving, unforgiving, slanderers, without self-control, brutal, despisers of good, traitors, headstrong, haughty, lovers of pleasure rather than lovers of God, having a form of godliness but denying its power. And from such people turn away! For of this sort are those who creep into households and make captives of*

gullible women loaded down with sins, led away by various lusts, always learning and never able to come to the knowledge of the truth.

—2 Timothy 3:1-7

That is a severe verdict of the human condition. The consequences of lawlessness are that the heart has less and less capacity to bounce back positively. Peoples' love tank is running on empty. There is still a lot being said about the mystical notion of love, but what are the results? I often hear the following reflection: "It is becoming harder and harder to love my neighbor."

Is there a need to add to the misery laid out in Paul's verses? No, I'll leave it at that.

But as the days of Noah were, so also will the coming of the Son of Man be.

—Matthew 24:37

That is a neutral statement. It could leave us wondering what this sentence means. *Noah*, the Russell Crowe film from 2014, got many, but not all, details about the flood right. In the movie, Noah's family was awash in a sea of wickedness. This lines up with what the Holy Scriptures say:

Then the Lord saw that the wickedness of man was great in the earth, and that every intent of the thoughts of his heart was only evil continually. And the Lord was sorry that He had made man on the earth, and He was grieved in His heart.

—Genesis 6:5-6

Do you remember the days when people believed that humanity was essentially good in nature? The speculation about man being basically good has been changing. Of course, we still see daily acts of love and kindness that inspire! But, as times become more terrifying, the human heart's capacity to rebound positively will significantly diminish. The previous verses give us an overview of where we are headed. But I think I just heard someone cry out that we are already there.

We have an excellent television in our house, and you probably do, also. Whenever we go through the hundreds of nightly offerings, it is sad to note the few program offerings of any moral value. Violence, blatant sexual immorality, addiction in many flavors, and corruption fill the nightly programming. Internet offerings stretch the limits even more. Excuse me for saying it; this is sickening for the heart, and is a clear indication of mankind's wickedness. Surely, God is grieved by us.

In the previous chapter, numerous points from Matthew 24 were shared that are now accepted as fact. They have happened and are happening, and for the sake of brevity I have not included all the signs that Jesus referred to. The world, in general, either doesn't believe or is not aware of what Jesus prophesied. It is time to examine more essential points recorded in Matthew 24.

DESTRUCTION OF THE TEMPLE

Jesus predicts the destruction of the temple in Jerusalem:

> *Then Jesus went out and departed from the temple, and His disciples came up to show Him the buildings of the temple. And Jesus said to them, "Do you not see all these things? Assuredly, I say to you, not one stone shall be left here upon another, that shall not be thrown down."*
>
> —Matthew 24:1–2

These verses don't fall into a neat category of what people generally accept as having occurred, but a quote from The Pulpit Commentary, a highly regarded Bible reference, explains it in such a way that should dispel the confusion:

> *"Our Lord, in turn, calls attention to the glorious structure [of the Temple] to give added emphasis to his weighty denunciation. Not be left here one stone upon another. This*

prophecy was most literally fulfilled. Recent explorations have shown that not a stone of Herod's Temple remains in situ. The orders of Titus [Roman Emperor], given with regret, for the total demolition of the walls of temple and city, were carried out with cruel exactness, so that, as Josephus testifies, passers by would not have supposed that the place had ever been inhabited."[7]

In the ancient world, the temple in Jerusalem was a well-known landmark. But, who could possibly prophesy the destruction of the Hebrew temple? Jesus! Imagine if someone prophesied that the U.S. Capitol building in the United States or the Houses of Parliament in the United Kingdom would be totally dismantled. Hey, that's hard to believe! We might assume the person is a false prophet. Complicated? No! This cornerstone of Matthew's prophetic chapter started out with a **bang**.

It is a historical fact that the Hebrew temple was actually destroyed by the Romans in 70 AD. If the beginning of this prophecy has come true, we should be able to trust the rest of it, shouldn't we? The fulfillment of this particular prophecy directly impacted the lives of tens of thousands of people. Jews and Christians alike were scattered abroad. We know this to be true. Shouldn't we expect that the other prophecies in the same discourse will fall into place in like manner? This confidence should affect our faith, giving us hope in times of trial, making all that follows in Matthew relevant. For early Christians, the words of Jesus gave them faith and hope to confront their coming problems. We can do the same! Read on!

WHAT EXACTLY WILL "END," AND WHEN?

> *Now as He sat on the Mount of Olives, the disciples came to Him privately, saying, "Tell us, when will these things be? And what will be the sign of your coming, and of the end of the age?*
>
> —Matthew 24:3

I'm hoping that you noticed the last word in that quote was "…the end of the **age**" and not "the end of the **world**." Numerous translations of the Bible use the expression "end of the world." Still, allow me to get a bit theological. The word "**world**" used here has also been translated to mean "**time**" or "**age**."[8] More modern versions of the Bible tend to use the expression, "end of time." All of this is to say, the prophecy can be interpreted to mean the end of an age, or an era in time, rather than the complete destruction of the planet. The apostle Peter used slightly different language to explain the event:

> *…that He may send Jesus Christ, who was preached to you before, whom heaven must receive until the times of restoration of all things, which God has spoken by the mouth of all His holy prophets since the world began.*
>
> —Acts 3:20-21

No one really knows if it refers to a particular day or hour; however, we may have an indication of the general time, period, or framework within which the apocalypse would fall. Many want to know, "when will this happen?" Again, Jesus specifically told his disciples that no one can know the exact day or hour.

> *But of that day and hour no one knows, not even the angels of heaven, but My Father only.*
>
> —Matthew 24:36

Major pothole alert! The end of the world concept is expressed in various ways in different Bible translations, but don't think about this as the annihilation of the world. The prophecy is very clear. This is not the end! The question is not "when" the apocalypse will happen. The question is, "what happens after Armageddon?" **Jesus never said that the world would "end" at his**

return! We *do* have reason to hope! We do *not* need to live in a fatalistic mentality.

CHAPTER 3

NATURAL DISASTERS AND PROPHECY

Now that we have looked at man-made events, let's look at natural events foretold many ages ago:

PLAGUES

> *For nation will rise against nation, and kingdom against kingdom. And there will be famines, pestilences, and earthquakes in various places.*
>
> —Matthew 24:7

The Greek word used here for "pestilences" means a pest, a plague, an epidemic, or a pestilent fellow.[9] Or, by explanation: viruses that are beyond medical control—plagues that emerge from nowhere and are, until now, unknown to man. Sound familiar?

Here are some of the references to health menaces in the Book of Revelation (emphases mine):

> These have power to shut heaven, so that no rain falls in the days of their prophecy; and they have power over waters to turn them to blood, and to **strike the earth with all plagues**, as often as they desire.
> —Revelation 11:6

> So the first went and poured out his bowl upon the earth, and **a foul and loathsome sore came upon the men** who had the mark of the beast and those who worshiped his image.
> —Revelation 16:2

> Then the fifth angel poured out his bowl on the throne of the beast, and his kingdom became full of darkness; and they gnawed their tongues because of the pain. They blasphemed the God of heaven **because of their pains and their sores**, and did not repent of their deeds.
> —Revelation 16:10-11

Medical advancements provide hope that many diseases will be conquered. We indeed share this feeling! My life has been made easier and prolonged by numerous medical treatments and procedures I have undergone. I suspect that you can say as much. I am deeply grateful for these medical advancements.

However, nothing leads us to believe that medical science conquers the pestilence mentioned in the Bible. These plagues have a terrible reputation:

> *When He opened the fourth seal, I heard the voice of the fourth living creature saying, "Come and see." So I looked, and behold, a pale horse. And the name of him who sat on it was Death, and Hades followed with him. And power was given to them over a fourth of the earth, to kill with sword, with hunger, with death, and by the beasts of the earth.*
> —Revelation 6:7-8

These verses and the rest of Revelation 6 give the impression that these plagues, both through pestilence and in other forms, will, at some point in time, conquer humanity. These are not comfortable concepts, but do they seem to be a stretch of the imagination?

By Spring 2022, the light at the end of the coronavirus tunnel appears as a glimmer of light. By the time you read this, we may have already wiggled our way out. *But,* we indeed haven't seen the end of these viral threats to the human race.

What do these verses seem to say to you?

> *Then the fourth angel poured out his bowl on the sun, and power was given to him to scorch men with fire. And men were scorched with great heat, and they blasphemed the name of God who has power over these plagues; and they did not repent and give Him glory.*
>
> —Revelation 16:8-9

EARTHQUAKES, TSUNAMIS, AND VOLCANOES

You probably didn't feel the horrendous consequences of the 2004 tsunami in the Indian Ocean, but you certainly know that over 200,000 people lost their lives in the deadliest tsunami in recorded history.

> *For nation will rise against nation, and kingdom against kingdom. And there will be famines, pestilences, and earthquakes in various places.*
>
> —Matthew 24:7

> *I looked when He opened the sixth seal, and behold, there was a great earth-*

quake; and the sun became black as sackcloth of hair, and the moon became like blood.

—Revelation 6:12

According to the National Oceanic and Atmospheric Administration (NOAA) 95% of all tsunamis are caused by underwater earthquakes. Earthquakes are not unusual, but the NOAA tells us their frequency and severity is increasing dramatically. NOAA data over the last four decades shows the frequency of tsunamis has increased 10 fold since the 1990s. In the 10 years since 2004, the Geological Society of America reported the number of "great quakes," measuring 8.0 or higher on the Richter scale, increased 265%.[10] The tsunami that hit Tonga on January 15, 2022 was unusual in that both an underwater volcanic explosion and earthquake occurred simultaneously.

Perhaps you don't live in a coastal city, or near an active volcano or fault line. These sorts of natural events do not touch you—but could they? Our city, Mulhouse, France, is twinned with Walsall, England. My wife and I were excited to be going to England. We were part of a delegation sent to Walsall by our local churches. We got up about 4 a.m. and did all we could to leave on time. But, something went wrong on that early morning of April 14, 2010. As we gathered together to leave, we heard on the news that the unpronounceable Eyjafjallajökull volcano had erupted "causing enormous disruption to air travel. Much of Europe closed their airspace to commercial jet traffic, canceling over 100,000 flights and affecting approximately ten million travelers."[11]

We had never seen anything like this, and the whole world looked on with us. So, we drove and drove, ferried to England, and then we drove some more. Arriving in Walsall twenty-four hours later, we were personally affected by this volcano. All this provoked us to think of the sun being covered with a black veil, as previously mentioned in Revelation 6:12.

Both volcanoes and tsunamis are different results of earthquakes. After all, they all share a common base—the trembling of the earth.

> *[Theory:* I believe that earthquakes will continue to increase in number and intensity. The experts are currently debating when the next "big one" will happen. We shall see. We do know that we can expect one particular shaking of more than our planet. Is the following prophecy literal or metaphorical? What do you think? Either way, there's going to be "A Whole Lotta Shakin' Going On" (thanks, Jerry Lee Lewis).]

> *But now He has promised, saying, "Yet once more I shake not only the earth, but also heaven."*
>
> —Hebrews 12:26

A MONSTER METEORITE

It seems appropriate to bring in a few scriptures at this time:

> *Then the third angel sounded: And a great star fell from heaven, burning like a torch, and it fell on a third of the rivers and on the springs of water. The name of the star is Wormwood. A third of the waters became wormwood, and many men died from the water, because it was made bitter.*
>
> —Revelation 8:10-11

Prophecy says a giant asteroid will hit the earth and poison our waters. Wormwood is an ancient word for bitterness. Modern linguists would put it this way; a meteor will impact the planet, and a third of the water will become undrinkable. That is not me speaking, but the Bible. Numerous movies have used the theme. I wonder if the apostle John should receive royalties from the box office sales. His text is where these movies got the idea!

The apostle John also shared other predictions

about fire, drought, and a description of things to come that boggles the mind:

> *Then the angel took the censer, filled it with fire from the altar, and threw it to the earth. And there were noises, thunderings, lightnings, and an earthquake. So the seven angels who had the seven trumpets prepared themselves to sound. The first angel sounded: And hail and fire followed, mingled with blood, and they were thrown to the earth. And a third of the trees were burned up, and all green grass was burned up.*
>
> —Revelation 8:5-7

John said other things that remain a mystery. Who can say exactly what this means?

> *The shape of the locusts was like horses prepared for battle. On their heads were crowns of something like gold, and their faces were like the faces of men. They had hair like women's hair, and their teeth were like lions' teeth. And they had breastplates like breastplates of iron, and the sound of their wings was like the sound of chariots with many horses running into battle. They had tails like scorpions, and there were*

stings in their tails. Their power was to hurt men five months.

—Revelation 9:7-10

[**Theory**: *The planet earth will increasingly go through incredibly bizarre natural phenomena. Geological and meteorological events our kind has never before experienced will be commonplace. "Wow, we have never seen that before," will be a common thought, and will signal other things to come. Regretfully, those "other things" aren't going to be a planetary birthday party.]*

What will we do? One or more cataclysms may come upon us by surprise. We will undoubtedly make Herculean efforts to save ourselves in crunch time. Yes, it will get hard!

So far, we have not heard very much hope, have we? In fact, there is more bad news ahead. But keep reading! Hope and a solution to all your doomsday fears are up ahead!

CHAPTER 4

THE TRAIL OF THE ANTICHRIST

And Jesus answered and said to them: "Take heed that no one deceives you. For many will come in My name, saying, "I am the Christ," and will deceive many.

—Matthew 24:4-5

Then if anyone says to you, "Look, here is the Christ!" or "There!" do not believe it. For false christs and false prophets will rise and show great signs and wonders to deceive, if possible, even the elect. See, I have told you beforehand. Therefore if they say to you, "Look, He is in the desert!" do not go out; or "Look, He is in the inner rooms!" do not believe it.

—Matthew 24:23-26

Jesus said that the most prominent sign of the end of the age was the multiplication of false prophets and false Christs. He repeated these warnings. When Jesus spoke repetitively, we need to pay special attention to what he said. That was his way of underlining the point he wanted to make. But, the world appears little concerned about false prophets and false Christs. Why should they be, when many people are eagerly following these modern-day "pied pipers of Hamelin?"

> *Little children, it is the last hour; and as you have heard that the Antichrist is coming, even now many antichrists have come, by which we know that it is the last hour.*
> —1 John 2:18

John announces that antichrists were active and were still to come. The same apostle speaks of dragons and beasts in Revelation 13. In one way or another, these beasts and dragons point to **one man—*the* Antichrist**. He will unite the religious, social, political, and economic systems into a world-dominating organization.

Sadly, the Church doesn't cease to spill out crazy theories concerning details about the Antichrist. We are always on the look-out for him! Consider the following commonly accepted expectations of the Antichrist extracted primarily from Revelation:

THE ANTICHRIST WILL ESTABLISH A RELIGIOUS SYSTEM.

This has not happened yet. However, for many centuries, numerous Christian churches have accused the Roman Catholic Church of being the seat of power of the Antichrist. Don't be shocked. This accusation is recorded in our history books. The Church of Rome also launched counter-accusations against a wide pallet of Christian denominations. Many pseudo-religious organizations have also been tagged as connected to the Antichrist: Templar, Illuminati, Masons, secret societies, and even flying saucer cults. From your personal experience, you can probably add to the list. In the end, almost all religious groups have been accused, at least once, of being the Antichrist. Yet, the real one is still to come!

THE ANTICHRIST NEEDS A SOCIAL SYSTEM TO RULE THE WORLD.

This also has not happened yet. Several social structures have been labeled as being part of the Antichrist's scheme. I'll insert **theories** (not mine) right here. None of these systems merit the title of Antichrist. Still, they have helped speed up the eventual establishment of a one-world system. They have made it easier to track every man, woman, and child on the planet. Those social systems include, but are not limited to:

The Social Security System is thought by some to be of the Antichrist. When the Social

Security Act was enacted in 1935 by Franklin D. Roosevelt, it sent countless Christians into a tither. They imagined that their social security number was the mark of the beast. America was one of the first countries to launch such a system, but virtually the entire world has followed suit. Almost everyone in the world has been given a number by their government. Don't think this to be a criticism of the Social Security system.

Modern technological advances such as geo-localization, QR codes, microchips and nanotechnology are believed by some to be tools of the Antichrist that will someday empower his social systems. As you read this, your microchip credit card is probably in your pants pocket or purse, right? You use it daily to buy and sell. Without it, life could become more complicated. Next on the agenda: do you fear nanobots are coming to get you? Digital, genetic tracing is coming at us straight out of the future. All of this is coming together at the same point in time. It is bizarre and we should pay attention—but read on! You have no reason to fear.

THE ANTICHRIST WILL BE THE ESTABLISHED WORLDWIDE POLITICAL LEADER, CREATING THE "NEW ONE-WORLD ORDER."

This has not yet happened! However, from the beginning of time, men have dreamed of ruling the world. You know some of their names: Alexander the Great, Genghis Khan, Napoleon, Hitler, Stalin, even down to our present-day mad-man, Kim Jong-un. Many have been offended to have been left off this list. **What does the "New One-World Order" really mean?**

According to Revelation 13, the Antichrist will usher in a universal economic system. Verses 16-18 give us an outline of the coming system:

> *He causes all, both small and great, rich and poor, free and slave, to receive a mark on their right hand or on their foreheads, and that no one may buy or sell except one who has the mark or the name of the beast, or the number of his name... Here is wisdom. Let him who has understanding calculate the number of the beast, for it is the number of a man: His number is 666.*
>
> —Revelation 13:16-18

These verses lead us to believe that the world's political and economic systems will merge for one simple objective: domination and control of the world. We are the first generation that is seeing such a system emerge. Most of the Western world is almost at the point where this can happen. Amazingly, the developing world is not far behind.

I vividly remember a college professor's question in class one day: "What technological invention has most impacted the world since World War II?" We all thought we knew or could, at least, make a noble guess. We were all wrong! His answer floored us: It was the transistor radio! During the class, we learned that the transistor democratized technology for the entire world. My professor's closing statement capped it all: *"Even the poor, illiterate Egyptian peasant sitting by the side of a dusty road could hear news from all over the world."*

Since then, the computer and smart phones probably have had the same impact. People in Sierra Leone, Canada, Greenland, or any spot you choose, all have computers—or at least cell phones. Connectedness makes the economic identification system possible. That couldn't have been imagined in the Middle Ages. Today, wherever you travel with your cell phone, **BAM**, you are geolocalized.

THE ANTICHRIST WILL BE A HUMAN—AND MALE.

Has he been born yet? No one knows. There have been so many wild predictions about who specifically the Antichrist might be that it is exasperating! Let us stick to a few of those guesses that are easily recognizable in modern times: The Pope (all of them), Martin Luther, Napoleon, Rasputin, Hitler, Mao, Charles Manson, Bill Clinton, Jared Kushner (Donald Trump's son-in-law), Bill Gates…and the next one up is…?

All these men share one feature: They all had or currently have immense power. People argue that some of these men wielded that power in blatantly wicked ways. Some used that power in a secretive manner. Still, others were nobler in their use of power. Somewhere out in the cosmos, all of these names have been cited as the potential Antichrist. I'm not smart enough to invent such a list or figure out who "*the* **man**" is. Someday the entire world will know. Is it soon?

In **Revelation 13**, we see the exploits of the man known as the Antichrist:

Verse 3: *"And I saw one of his heads as if it had been mortally wounded, and his deadly wound was healed. And all the world marveled and followed the beast."*

Verse 5: *"And he was given a mouth speaking great things and blasphemies, and he was given authority to continue for forty-two months."*

Verse 7: *It was granted to him to make war with the saints and to overcome them. And authority was given him over every tribe, tongue, and nation.* ("Saints" here is commonly interpreted as all believing Christians, not particularly those that have been sainted).

Verse 8: *"All who dwell on the earth will worship him, whose names have not been written in the Book of Life of the Lamb slain from the foundation of the world."*

Verse 13-14: *"He performs great signs, so that*

he even makes fire come down from heaven on the earth in the sight of men. And he deceives those who dwell on the earth by those signs which he was granted to do in the sight of the beast, telling those who dwell on the earth to make an image to the beast who was wounded by the sword and lived."

The Bible shows us that the Antichrist has quite a program. Other traits include him being a man of lawlessness and performing mighty miracles. This is developed elsewhere, but there is simply too much to include here.

Now it is time to consider how everything comes together.

CHAPTER 5

BIRTH PANGS OF A NEW WORLD

"All these are the beginning of sorrows."
—Matthew 24:8

"The beginning of sorrows" doesn't sound very hopeful, does it? Yet, Psalms 30:5 reminds us to look ahead:

For His anger is but for a moment, His favor is for life; Weeping may endure for a night, but joy comes in the morning.

So, what comes next? What is the overall picture?

[**Theory**: *I believe that we are at a crossroads where these events start coming in series. When you consider all these vexing events together, it seems that the force and frequency are increasing.*

Can we be at the point in time that the apostle Paul spoke of in Romans 8:22?]

> *"For we know that the whole creation groans and labors with birth pangs together until now."*

Ask an ecologist if he thinks that the earth is groaning. What do you think his answer be? How does that answer compare with what I have just shared?

From conception, a woman's body goes through periods of painful and uncomfortable change. The Church can be compared to a pregnant woman. Over the years, the Church has gone through multiple periods of discomfort. These periods all point to the awaited arrival. What is that arrival?

I'm not an expert in childbirth, so I asked Elisa, a young mother I know, to share her experience:

> *"At the beginning, before leaving for the maternity ward, I had some contractions every 20 minutes or so. They were painful, but it was okay. They didn't last very long.*
>
> *Then the contractions got closer and closer and became more and more painful and more prolonged. When contractions become more intense, you have to relax. You have to "surf" on the contraction, let it run*

its course, and not get tense. Basically, the more imminent the delivery, the more the contractions are closer together and the more intense they are."

Like Elisa's personal experience, will the painful labor pains of the earth accelerate until there is a delivery?

THE QUESTIONS

For they are spirits of demons, performing signs, which go out to the kings of the earth and of the whole world, to gather them to the battle of that great day of God Almighty.

"Behold, I am coming as a thief. Blessed is he who watches, and keeps his garments, lest he walk naked and they see his shame."

And they gathered them together to the place called in Hebrew, Armageddon.

—Revelation 16:14-16

We also need to see what a few prophets and apostles said about events that will happen during the apocalypse. Remember, we are using the terms "apocalypse" and "Armageddon" interchangeably as they refer to the same event, which brings me to an important point.

WILL THERE BE AN ACTUAL "MAIN EVENT"?

Immediately after the tribulation of those days, the sun will be darkened. The moon will not give its light; the stars will fall from heaven, and the powers of the heavens will be shaken. Then the sign of the Son of Man will appear in heaven, and then all the tribes of the earth will mourn, and they will see the Son of Man coming on the clouds of heaven with power and great glory. And He will send His angels with a great sound of a trumpet, and they will gather together His elect from the four winds, from one end of heaven to the other.

—Matthew 24:29-31

Yes, there will be an actual battle. Spoiler alert: Jesus wins! It is next to impossible to grasp the magnitude of what is happening here. Steven Spielberg is the master of special effects, but what you just read tops everything that Steven and all his buddies have been able to put on the screen. It is fantastic! Jesus will gather unto himself *everyone in the entire world that has called upon his name.*

IS ARMAGEDDON A REAL PLACE?

The mystical Armageddon is a name to describe a real place in the world that does exist. The word has no connection to the film of that title from 1998: a world-saving asteroid-busting mission. There is little wonder why people are confused about some biblical words and names.

Megiddo (Hebrew: Har Megiddo) is a small city in north-central Israel, on the southern edge of the Plain of Esdraelon. Many historians predict this strategic military position would be the perfect place for the ultimate battle.

The few lines about Armageddon in the book of Revelation tell a morbid story. It is the last battlefield for the confrontation of the forces of good and evil. The logistics are massively shocking:

Now the number of the army of the horsemen was two hundred million; I heard the number of them.

—Revelation 9:16

The eventual victory coincides with the return of Jesus Christ to planet Earth!

Let's get the observation about Armageddon from a war professional, General Douglas MacArthur, from his farewell speech to the American Congress on April 19, 1951:

"Men since the beginning of time have sought peace. Various methods through the ages have been attempted to devise an international process to prevent or settle dis-

> *putes between nations. From the very start, workable methods were found insofar as individual citizens were concerned, but the mechanics of an instrumentality of larger international scope have never been successful. Military alliances, balances of power, Leagues of Nations, all, in turn failed, leaving the only path to be by way of the crucible of war. The utter destructiveness of war now blocks out this alternative. We have had our last chance. If we do not devise some greater and more equitable system, Armageddon will be at our door. The problem basically is theological and involves a spiritual recrudescence and improvement of human character that will synchronize with our almost matchless advances in science, art, literature, and all material and cultural developments of the past 2000 years. It must be of the spirit if we are to save the flesh."[12]*

Armageddon represents the final war in about anybody's book. **It is**, but you have to keep on reading to see that it isn't "**la fin!**"

The finality and hopelessness of how the end of the world is depicted in movies and other media does not correspond with what the Bible reveals! We will see these tragic events. All this is happening, but not because we drive too many polluting cars or we use too much wasteful plastic. Sure, these are significant problems. But this is happening because the heart of man has become more and more egoist.

That is the primary issue, so let me repeat it:

The condition of mankind's heart has become so self-centered that greed, violence, domination, and indifference to our fellow man have blinded the world to God's Word and placed our feet on the path to destruction.

Bottom line: The world we currently live in will be destroyed.

But, this is not the end of the story. The Bible paints a beautiful picture of what is to follow.

No more tears, no more political corruption, ravaging sicknesses are banished, no more wars or even rumors of wars. We will be able to breathe, eat, and drink without fear. What humanity cries out for will happen because Jesus Christ will return to earth to rule.

WHOM SHALL WE FEAR?

What do you fear the most? Do you fear this day of destruction? Do you fear the world will completely disappear?

Listen, the world will not be destroyed to make room for a vast nothingness.

I apologize for the massive clash of ideas presented here. You may have to reflect on these words to grasp their significance.

That is not one of my theories but a biblical proclamation. The Bible declares that there are other, very positive things going on at the same time. Ready to move on to your biggest question?

WHEN WILL ARMAGEDDON HAPPEN?

> *"But of that day and hour no one knows, not even the angels of heaven, but My Father only."*
>
> —Matthew 24:36

A prediction flashes across the Internet to announce, "The World Will End Next Thursday at 12:30 PM!" When I see assertions like this, I say to myself, "Doesn't anybody read the Bible?" There is nothing in the Holy Scriptures that encourages date-setting. Jesus was explicit: ONLY the Father knows when this will happen! A lot can be distilled out of that short proclamation. Flashback to **Matthew 24:3:**

> *Now as He sat on the Mount of Olives, the disciples came to Him privately, saying, "Tell us, when will these things be? And what will be the sign of Your coming, and of the end of the age?"*

A paradox comes crashing down upon us. Imagine the followers' question in modern lingo: "Come on, Jesus, when is all this stuff going to happen? Please give us a clue because we want to be in the loop."

With all the details Jesus gave to them, and now to us, he established the **general** framework of when we should expect the apocalypse. Could this be that time?

> *So you also, when you see all these things, know that it is near—at the doors! Assuredly, I say to you, this generation will by no means pass away till all these things take place. Heaven and earth will pass away, but My words will by no means pass away.*
> —Matthew 24:33-35

Jesus explained the general timing of the wrap-up of the age, but he refused to give a date. Since this is true, what is the attitude that should guide us?

There is an adage which says, "Even if I knew that tomorrow the world would go to pieces, I would still plant my apple tree."

What does this mean? Anyone who can utter these words is at peace with himself, God, and the future. There is no stress in this wise saying. I want to adopt this attitude, particularly when I consider the birth pangs of the new world and all that is ahead. Do you also?

In 2020 the word **cluster,** meaning a small

group of people or things close together, took on a particular nuance.

Almost all of the prophetic details mentioned have been happening throughout the ages. Wars? Yes! Famines? Certainly! Earthquakes? Of course! But they have been sporadic and not necessarily simultaneously visible in the entire world. **Now, there is a prophetic clustering of all these events at this point in time.** That singular point marks a significant difference with all previous ages. Is that obvious to you?

Be ready!

> *Watch therefore, for you do not know what hour your Lord is coming. But know this, that if the master of the house had known what hour the thief would come, he would have watched and not allowed his house to be broken into. Therefore you also be ready, for the Son of Man is coming at an hour you do not expect.*
>
> —Matthew 24:42-44

Every time I prepare for a long flight, I have a poor night's sleep. I'm in a state of enthusiastic anticipation. Of the hundreds of flights I have taken, I have missed only one. That was a terrible experience. Now, I want to be sure all the details are correct—even perfect. When it all comes together and I get on the plane, I usually fall asleep. This is true!

With all that is happening, the world wants to go to sleep *without being prepared!* Christians are called to be wide-eyed and bushy-tailed until he returns. Yes, I want to be ready for the return of Jesus Christ. Regretfully, there are fewer and fewer churches teaching this aspect of the Gospel. Whatever background you are from, I encourage you to join me in preparation for that **great day**.

PART II

ARMAGEDDON AND THE CHURCH

Up until this point, we have been talking about what to expect in the *world,* but what about the Church? And what about the Jewish people? At the very beginning of this little book I asked one thing of you: to make peace with your relationship with the Church. You are about to learn why this is so important. You are about to come face to face with the reality of today's broken Church and the promise of healing and the important role the Church will play in the end times.

The Bible speaks of the Church, and the

Church often speaks of the Bible. The Bible is the plumb line for the Church, not the inverse. The Bible always trumps man-made traditions. But, the Church cannot be separated from the prophecies we are studying. What, or who, is "the Church," and how does the Church figure into the prophecies about Armageddon?

CHAPTER 6

THE CHURCH DEFINED

WHAT, OR WHO, IS "THE CHURCH"?

When the word **Church** is used in this text, it always refers to **all Christian denominations**. The word **church** (without capitals) refers to a local assembly or assemblies. The concept of Church goes from Copts to Catholics; from Pentecostals to Presbyterians; Messianic Judaism to Methodists; from Brethren to Lutherans; all the independents, in China, in Africa, in America or Europe; from Eastern Catholics to the Orthodox; from Anglicans to Baptists; from Quakers to Shakers. Not everybody on the list would appreciate the company of the others. They need to grin and bear it; they are still part of the family.

I made a serious effort to include everyone, but a complete list is impossible because the gospel seed has been scattered far and wide. When you add up the entire family tree, you reach a **total worldwide Christian population of 2.6 billion.**[13]

The Apostles Creed is a thread that runs

through almost all Christian denominations. There are slight variations in the wording in some denominations, but the content does not change. In many churches, it is recited as part of the Sunday gathering of the believers. Let us take a look up close:

> *I believe in God, the Father almighty, creator of heaven and earth.*
>
> *I believe in Jesus Christ, God's only Son, our Lord, who was conceived by the Holy Spirit, born of the Virgin Mary, suffered under Pontius Pilate, was crucified, died, and was buried; he descended to the dead.*
>
> *On the third day he rose again; he ascended into heaven, he is seated at the right hand of the Father, and he will come to judge the living and the dead.*
>
> *I believe in the Holy Spirit, the holy catholic Church, the communion of saints, the forgiveness of sins, the resurrection of the body, and the life everlasting. Amen.*

One notable difference is the word catholic. The word catholic in the text is not the same as Roman Catholic. "Universal" replaces the word "catholic" at times. The root word is the same but translated differently. But, please note a critical line: "*...and he [Jesus] will come to judge the living and the dead.*"

One of the foundational truths of the Christian churches of the world lies in this statement, found in 2 Timothy 4:1—that Jesus Christ will come again *to judge the living and the dead.*

THE CHURCH DIVIDED

When you think about the Church, you may picture a lot of individual churches divided into groups of matching theologies. Instead, think about the people in all the world who identify themselves as Christians. We're going to divide those people into just three groups.

I warned you about potholes, and I want to signal the presence of one right before us. Many of the 2.6 billion people who identify themselves as being Christian do not truly understand what it means to be a Christian, or truly understand and believe who Jesus Christ is. Many, then, are unaware that Jesus is coming back. Here we have an oxymoron: there are many, many **unbelieving "believers."** Don't imagine that this was said in a critical spirit because it is merely **a fact**. Multitudes who believe they are Christians do not know or believe in the basic, Biblical tenets of the Christian faith. You may be in this camp. I am not judging you! You are not alone! Many in this position inherited their religious beliefs and practices from their parents.

Others have simply never examined the Bible or their own beliefs for themselves, allowing their peers and the culture around them to decide for them what they believe. They are distracted, perhaps complacent—that is, until they suffer a loss or are faced with a fear they cannot process. Then, they might pick up this little book. Perhaps this is why you are reading it now. I am here to help you, my friend!

In that same 2.6 billion number, there is also a crowd that denies that Jesus will return. That usually, but not always, accompanies beliefs that Jesus was not divine, that he was not God's own son, but just a man.

So, the Universal Church is divided into three points of view concerning the return of Jesus Christ to judge the living and the dead:

1. Those that believe and await the return of Jesus Christ.
2. Those that are unaware of his return.
3. Those that deny his return will occur.

You see that things can get complicated. In another chapter we will talk briefly about another common way the Church has been fractured: denominations.

THE CHURCH PERSECUTED

> *Then they will deliver you up to tribulation and kill you, and you will be hated by all*

nations for My name's sake. And then many will be offended, will betray one another, and will hate one another. Then many false prophets will rise up and deceive many. And because lawlessness will abound, the love of many will grow cold. But he who endures to the end shall be saved.

—Matthew 24:9-13

People who don't identify themselves as Christians often don't know about the persecution of Christians. This isn't because of bad press; it is because of zero press. The media doesn't cover this type of story. But, from time to time, a story trickles out of a press room here or there.

Ewelina U. Ochab wrote in a recent article, "Persecuted Christians Are Not Given Much Hope In 2020":

"In January 2020, Open Doors, an international NGO (non-governmental organization) advocating on behalf of persecuted Christians, released their annual report. The World Watch List 2020 does not give much hope for the persecuted communities. Indeed, it presents a grim picture of Christians' situation globally, making it very clear that the persecution encountered by them continues to worsen. The report identifies that 'in 2020, 260 million Christians live in World Watch

List top 50 countries where Christians are at risk of high, very high or extreme levels of persecution. This is up from 245 million in 2019.' The report also emphasizes some important, negative changes within global trends of the persecution of Christians."[14]

Ochab went on to report that more than 5,500 churches by that point in time had been shuttered, broken up, or taken over by the government. In the year 2019, she accounted for roughly 1500 assaults and death threats, and well over 1,000 Christians in Nigeria were murdered for their faith. "Indeed, these numbers do not give much hope to the persecuted," she commented.

This type of persecution hasn't been seen in the West, but many believe it may soon come.

The effects of all of the above on the human heart are:

And because lawlessness will abound, the love of many will grow cold. But he who endures to the end shall be saved.
—Matthew 24:12-13

Maybe this would be an excellent time to bring in another set of signs from the epistles of Paul:

But know this, that in the last days perilous times will come: For men will be lovers of themselves, lovers of money, boasters, proud, blasphemers, disobedient to parents, unthankful, unholy, unloving, unforgiving, slanderers, without self-control, brutal, despisers of good, traitors, headstrong, haughty, lovers of pleasure rather than lovers of God, having a form of godliness but denying its power. And from such people turn away!

—2 Timothy 3:1-5

THE CHURCH DIVERSIFIED

Do you want to know when Armageddon will come? Here is another clue:

And this gospel of the kingdom will be preached in all the world as a witness to all the nations, and then the end will come.
—Matthew 24:14

Has the gospel been preached in all the world yet? Jacob Westland from Pioneers Europe, a church-planting ministry since 1998, says, "definitely not," claiming there are billions left who have never heard about Jesus. Here is the great commission:

And Jesus came and spoke to them, saying, "All authority has been given to

Me in heaven and on earth. Go therefore and make disciples of all the nations, baptizing them in the name of the Father and of the Son and of the Holy Spirit, teaching them to observe all things that I have commanded you; and lo, I am with you always, even to the end of the age.

—Matthew 28:18-20

Westland made the following observation:

Although by now the gospel has gone to all countries (nations), this is not what Jesus meant when he ordered his followers to make disciples of all nations. In Matthew 28:18-20, Jesus was not referring to nations such as Canada, Kenya, or Russia. The word that Jesus used for nations is the Greek word "ethne," from which the English word "ethnic" is derived. "Ethne" means a group of people with a common identity, such as the same language, culture, religion, or ethnicity. In the Great Commandment, Jesus ordered his followers to make disciples of every ethnic group, every people group. For example, Nigeria is one nation but has 540 different ethnic groups.[15]

Soon it will be possible that every ethnic group in the world will hear the gospel. They will be able to choose for themselves if they want to become followers of Christ.

CHAPTER 7

THE CHURCH IN THE END TIMES

Amazing things are here, waiting to be discovered, but a few potholes are also coming.

What is your vision of the Church as a whole? Where is the Church going? Is she relevant in the modern world? Do you even go to church? I can only try to imagine all of your answers.

I suspect most people feel that the Church is like a pinball game. The chrome ball comes rolling down between the bumpers, and the objective is to score points on the way down. The ball ricochets right and left, and a flipper shoots the pinball back to the top. The Church seems to be bouncing around the world without any clear direction or purpose. Flipper shots are being made all the time to save the Church from ending up "out of play." Do you see the Church this way?

The Bible describes the Church in a totally different light. The end of the world and the story of the Church are intertwined. They cannot be separated. Hollywood spins tales about the end of the world, but they never include the Church in these scenarios. Never!

Let's be clear, Christians sometimes don't understand all that is explicitly written in the Bible. Unfortunately, the Church can be very forgetful. As a result, certain Bible truths have been ignored, some are denied, and others have just slipped away.

I grew up in a church that did not believe in Bible miracles or current-day miracles. Over the years, belief in the miraculous was escorted out the back door. Sadly, they had no understanding of how the miraculous works, historically or today.

You may not believe in miracles. That's OK! But when you take the miraculous out of the Bible, you also ask God to leave. After all, he is, by definition, a God of miracles. If he isn't, it should be clear that he could not be God. He would be no different than Joe, the fireman living down the street. For some, this idea is hard to understand! Maybe a speed bump. A pothole. As I asked at the beginning of this little book, when you encounter a pothole, drive around it. For now, suspend your disbelief in miracles and allow for the possibility that God is able to do the impossible!

The following is one such miracle that is hard for even me to believe! Remember, Jesus will gather unto himself *everyone in the entire world that has called upon his name.*

THE UNIFICATION OF THE CHURCH

Are we close to the end of the world? If we are, there is one crucial point that must come into focus. The Church must radically, profoundly, **drastically change** to be conformed to Bible texts! This will take a miracle, won't it?

Jesus offered up two prayers to God that we remember well.

> *Our Father in heaven, hallowed be your name.*
>
> *Your kingdom come.*
>
> *Your will be done on earth as it is in heaven.*
>
> *Give us this day our daily bread.*
>
> *And forgive us our debts, as we forgive our debtors.*
>
> *And do not lead us into temptation, but deliver us from the evil one.*
>
> *For Yours is the kingdom and the power and the glory forever. Amen.*
>
> —Matthew 6:9-13

Not everyone can recite this prayer by memory, but they at least know about it. In the second prayer, Jesus prayed for himself, for his disciples, and in the following passage, for Christians in future generations:

> *"I do not pray for these alone, but also for those who will believe in Me through their word; that they all may be one, as You, Father, are in Me, and I in You; that they also may be one in Us, that the world may believe that You sent Me. And the glory which You gave Me I have given them, that they may be one just as We are one: I in them, and You in Me; that they may be made perfect in one, and that the world may know that You have sent Me, and have loved them as You have loved Me."*

—John 17: 20-23

If you time-travel into the Church's past, you certainly won't see much that resembles what Jesus prayed for. Human nature is divisive, but divine nature is unifying. Sometimes the world screams at Christians, "If you're all serving the same God, why are there so many denominations?" Well said! I couldn't agree more. To the world, our division may seem like almost historical proof that God doesn't exist. You noticed the word **almost** inserted into the last sentence.

Jesus repeated the same prayer three times. He insisted, *"Father, make them **one**!"* I think that this is the only time Jesus repeated the same prayer **three** times. Is it reasonable to believe that his prayer will be answered? Someone somewhere will see this prayer answered. But it won't be just one person hidden on the backside of nowhere. Currently, Christianity is in shambles, but Jesus has prayed the Church up to another level. Believers will be perfectly one! Wow!!

How will this happen?

[**Theory**: *I believe that the Christian Church will be unified, but not in the way most would imagine. The following is how I interpret what the Bible says about the unification of the Church.]*

Churches have their individual agendas, their members, their buildings, their budgets, and their identities. But God is bigger than all that.

When Christians understand that they are called to be one, they will realize that they will have to lay down their lives one for another. The Bible declares it. All the arguments in the world won't change that. The apostle Paul said it this way:

> *Therefore if there is any consolation in Christ, if any comfort of love, if any fellowship of the Spirit, if any affection and mercy, fulfill my joy by being like-minded,*

> *having the same love, being of one accord, of one mind.*
>
> *Let nothing be done through selfish ambition or conceit, but in lowliness of mind let each esteem others better than himself.*
>
> —Philippians 2:1-3

Only the God of miracles can perform this. He will do his part, but Christians must also do theirs. This is called **costly Christianity.** But, it was meant to be this way all along. Politics, personal ambition, money, sex, and power have corrupted the Church. She needs to come back to the naïve simplicity of loving God with her whole heart. And, loving her neighbor would not be a bad idea, either. No church is exempt from this. Please understand that God profoundly loves the Church, in all her brokenness, just as he loves each one of us.

The ecumenical movement has raised a vital question: "Are we really called to be one"? There has been progress toward unity, but the Church is still very far from the biblical vision of unity. Can this be achieved by the simple establishment of a "super Church" governmental structure? I think not. Instead, hearts need to beat together to the rhythm of the Father's heart. Jesus made it clear: "*This is My commandment, that you love one another as I have loved you.*" —John 15:12

One example of this type of unity came to us

from a communist Eastern Bloc country many years ago. Because of their faith, six church leaders, pastors and priests from different denominations, were arrested and jailed. The men had never met, but they had been in regular contact with each other by mail. At the same time, another curious fellow was jailed. He had the unique talent of forging any handwritten document better than a photocopy machine. The government was about to use his talent to forge letters from these pastors denouncing each other. The pastors were all in the same prison, but they did not cross paths.

The police interrogated the pastors, and each interview ended in the same manner; "We ask you to denounce a fellow pastor, or you will go to prison for life. Another pastor denounced you in this (forged) handwritten letter. Read it, and then do the same." Write a false accusation or go to prison for life—what a choice!

With much emotion, each pastor responded in precisely the same manner. "I see the letter, and I know Uri's handwriting. But something is wrong. He is my brother in Christ, and we love one another. It may be his handwriting, but it is not his heart. I refuse to denounce another pastor." Each pastor received the verdict: life in prison! That is committed love to Jesus Christ and to fellow Christians.

The detective that directed the interrogations sat through six men laying their lives on the line because of the love of Christ. This echoes John 13:35: *By this, all will know that you are My disciples, if you have love for one another.*

The detective broke under the power of love that he heard in the pastors' responses. The pastors were soon released, and the policeman followed them in their faith!

DENOMINATIONS

> *"To be, or not to be, that is the question!"*
> Hamlet, Act III, Scene I William Shakespeare

Many people wonder how the Church can unite with so many denominations. Others use their denominational background as an excuse, a way to get out of a conversation. What will happen with all of the denominations when the Church unites?

To join a denomination or not is a fundamental question. Which one is **best**? Are there any **worst** denominations? First, think about this: there is no single denomination mentioned in the Bible—not a verse, not a word, not a whisper. This statement may be hard to believe. After all, multitudes of denominational churches dot the countryside.

It would be understandable if your reaction to this statement was complicated. You may say to yourself: "It really doesn't matter. I know who I am, and I love my church."

Or, you may say: "I'm distraught. It seems I have been misled to believe that my church was the 'only' one, or the 'best' one. After all, we have the truth."

Or perhaps: "I'll have to think about all this. It is hard to digest."

The Bible talks about believers without any particular distinction between the uncountable multitudes. Christians are called *"a chosen generation, a royal priesthood, a holy nation, His own special people, that you may proclaim the praises of Him who called you out of darkness into His marvelous light, who once were not a people but are now the people of God, who had not obtained mercy but now have obtained mercy."*—1 Peter 2:9-10

So, will the Church become a melting pot? What is your reaction to this idea? Think about it!

So what will happen? This is half **theory** and half based on the **fact** that all believers in Christ are on equal footing before God.

Is God always against denominations?
That is not a pothole but an atomic bomb. The answer is probably yes and no. Why is God not against denominations? Denominations are like family names. Family names come from the region where people live, the history they have written, and the culture they know. There

is identity in them. The Lord respects our social, historical identity. He promises to speak to mankind in all their diverse dialects and identities. He respects humanity and every family name. In this manner, God is not against denominations.

Could God ever be against denominations?
Yes. What would happen if you go around and tell all your neighbors that your family name is *better* than theirs? You are free to do this, but you will have terrible relations with them. Can you understand that churches need to change their attitude? Some churches have more history, more money, or more members. All those things do not make them *better*. The organized Church should stop all its prideful ways; one day, its members will.

Arrogant denominational attitudes will cease among true believers. I'm very familiar with arrogance because it was a personal traveling companion of mine for a long time. When I understood the shame attached to that attitude, I cried out to the Lord to forgive me. And you? Do you have arrogance toward other churches? Or, is your own arrogance keeping you away from the Church?

As we approach Armageddon, the lifeblood of humility will run through the Church. If God is in the unity business, all Christians are included. Believers have a lot to lose as they walk this path of unity—but the gain will far outweigh the loss.

God will receive glory when Christians walk in harmony. Oh, happy day! Whether you are outside the Church or within, reflect on that. The world will be a different place.

In a moment we will return to the Church and examine what will happen when this broken body becomes whole again. But first, what does the Bible say about the Jews, and what is their relationship to the Church going to be? What does that have to do with Armageddon?

CHAPTER 8

THE JEWISH RECONCILIATION

A short distance from my house, the earth opened up, and a hole the size of ten plus cars remained. Like the hole in my neighborhood, Jerusalem is like the monster pothole that can swallow you whole.

All the Christian world is not in agreement with the following point. But, you judge what the Bible says. There are hundreds of verses in the Old Testament that refer to Israel's return to her land. Controversy can start flying now. I would ask you to simply read what the Bible says on the subject:

> *For I will take you from among the nations, gather you out of all countries, and bring you into your own land. Then I will sprinkle clean water on you, and you shall be clean; I will cleanse you from all your*

filthiness and from all your idols. I will give you a new heart and put a new spirit within you; I will take the heart of stone out of your flesh and give you a heart of flesh. I will put My Spirit within you and cause you to walk in My statutes, and you will keep My judgments and do them.

Then you shall dwell in the land that I gave to your fathers; you shall be My people, and I will be your God. I will deliver you from all your uncleannesses. I will call for the grain and multiply it, and bring no famine upon you. And I will multiply the fruit of your trees and the increase of your fields, so that you need never again bear the reproach of famine among the nations. Then you will remember your evil ways and your deeds that were not good; and you will loathe yourselves in your own sight, for your iniquities and your abominations.

—Ezekiel 36:24-31

Let's try to isolate the elements of Ezekiel's prophecy:

ISRAEL WILL BE GATHERED FROM THE NATIONS.

True or false? Never in history have people come together from all over the world to recreate a country. Never! Israel, as a government, had ceased for 19 centuries. The Jewish people were swept this way and that for many, many lifetimes. In the end, they are coming back home!

GOD WILL CLEANSE THEIR HEARTS.

True or false? Many governments do not consider Israel as a country. Add to that, the Israeli government is known for numerous atrocities. No, they don't have a squeaky clean reputation. The spiritual nature of the return to the country is in contrast to the country's political reality. It appears any spiritual purification remains hidden. I'm just trying to be honest on all points.

ISRAEL WILL ENJOY AGRICULTURAL ABUNDANCE.

Israel is almost all desert land, with barely an inch of annual rainfall, and sun beating down all but a dozen days a year in the Negev Desert. Yet, the Bible tells us "crops will thrive, and the fruit trees will prosper." How is this possible? Are you aware of Israel's agricultural miracle? It is incredible!

> *The wilderness and the wasteland shall be glad for them, and the desert shall rejoice and blossom as the rose; it shall blossom abundantly and rejoice, even with joy and singing.*
>
> —Isaiah 35:1-2a

According to the Christian Science Monitor, for more than sixty years, Israeli agricultural technology has grown to produce enough food to both support their own population and export to other countries, far out-producing even the lush farmlands of the United States:

> *"Cotton yields in the Negev outstrip those of California, Arizona, and Egypt; peanut yields are four times higher than in Georgia and West Virginia…One farmer at Ein Yahav harvests crops three or four times a year, growing about 60 tons of food per acre - four to six times what a farmer in the United States might grow yearly."*[16]

All of this out of a formerly uninhabitable desert! Israel is sharing this life-saving technology worldwide to help farmers grow healthy crops even as the world becomes drier and hotter each decade. I cannot add to something said more than 2500 years ago.

JERUSALEM WILL BE A CURSE FOR ALL NATIONS.

> *Behold, I will make Jerusalem a cup of drunkenness to all the surrounding peoples when they lay siege against Judah and Jerusalem. And it shall happen in that day that I will make Jerusalem a very heavy stone for all peoples; all who would heave it away will*

surely be cut in pieces, though all nations of the earth are gathered against it.

—Zechariah 12:2-3

Not too many years ago, Jerusalem was a small city in the middle of the desert. In 2022, the city had a population approaching one million[17] and has become a major actor on the world stage. Jerusalem came out of relative obscurity to become, perhaps, the world's most hated city! This is not a subject of pride. Zechariah knew all about this. Again, we have a cluster of events concerning Israel that has never been seen before. Does this seem correct to you? Many, many books have been written on the subject.

JERUSALEM WILL MOURN FOR THE "PIERCED ONE."

And I will pour on the house of David and on the inhabitants of Jerusalem the Spirit of grace and supplication; then they will look on Me whom they pierced. Yes, they will mourn for Him as one mourns for his only son, and grieve for Him as one grieves for a firstborn.

—Zechariah 12:10

Controversy has seemed to always accompany Israel. Today, it has reached a high point. No matter what is said about Israel, you will find a contrary point of view. So, even my writing here is controversial!

The Jewish prophet Zechariah penned the above prophecy some five centuries before Jesus Christ was born. History points to one man that was pierced: Jesus. He was pierced when the **crown of thorns** was laid upon his head. He was pierced by **the nails driven through his hands and feet.** He was pierced **by a lance** that was thrust into his side. He was definitely **pierced**!

Zechariah said that God would pour a Spirit of grace and supplication on the house of David—this is the Jewish population—and also on *all* the inhabitants of Jerusalem. Right now, only a small portion of the Jewish population recognizes Jesus as the Son of God. This change will be God's doing! The result? The Jewish people and all inhabitants of Jerusalem will "*look on me whom they pierced.*" In uncomplicated English, this says that the Lord will pour out his Spirit on Jerusalem, and the inhabitants will mourn the Lord, whom they crucified. Their eyes will be opened! At this moment, the Church and the Jewish people will be one! Unimaginable! This must happen before Armageddon.

Zechariah's proclamations are hard to grasp. What I just wrote will probably cost me some friends.

This prophecy is like a two-stage missile. The lift-off was found in the last paragraph—a "man" was to be pierced. That was accomplished. The second stage comes much later, and has not occurred yet.

Was Zechariah writing to the inhabitants of Jerusalem who lived at the time of Jesus, or some time ahead? We do not know. The prediction also spoke of another phase concerning the inhabitants of Jerusalem. Who lives in Jerusalem now? Recent data says 64% of Jerusalem is Jewish, followed by 34% Muslim, and 2% Christian. The Jewish people have never recognized Jesus as their long-awaited Messiah, but one day, they will *"look on Me whom they pierced."* Yes, Zechariah tells us the Jewish people will mourn for Jesus as one mourns for his only Son.

Christian theology generally accepts that one day the Jewish nation will look upon "the Man they pierced." They will mourn his death. They will embrace the cross that he was put upon. They will accept that he was their Messiah! We just covered a long stretch of road here.

Try to imagine this: Zechariah gave this prophetic word in 500 B.C. It appears that, at the time of Christ, part of this prophecy was accomplished. Two thousand years later, the second phase comes into focus. A multi-phase prophecy is not uncommon in biblical prophecy. It is amazing!

A compliment and confirmation to the above verse:

> *But He was wounded [or pierced through] for our transgressions, He was bruised for our iniquities; the chastisement for our peace was upon Him, and by His stripes we are healed.*
>
> —Isaiah 53:5

THE OLIVE TREE OF THE LORD

In Romans 11, Israel was represented as an olive tree. The apostle Paul goes to great lengths to explain the history of this olive tree (author's explanations in brackets).

> *For if you [non-Jews] were cut out of the olive tree which is wild by nature, and were grafted contrary to nature into a cultivated olive tree [Israel], how much more will these [the Jewish nation cut off from the Messiah], who are natural branches, be grafted into their own olive tree?*
>
> *For I do not desire, brethren, that you should be ignorant of this mystery, lest you should be wise in your own opinion, that blindness in part has happened to Israel until the fullness of the Gentiles has come in. And so all Israel will be saved, as it is written:*
>
> *"The Deliverer will come out of Zion, And He will turn away ungodliness from*

> *Jacob; for this is My covenant with them, When I take away their sins."*
>
> *Concerning the gospel they are enemies for your sake, but concerning the election they are beloved for the sake of the fathers. For the gifts and the calling of God are irrevocable.*
>
> —Romans 11:24-29

Jesus Christ came to Israel as the Savior they had waited for. At that time, many Jews accepted him as such. All the apostles and the vast majority of the early Christians were Jewish. But, as a whole, Israel rejected Christ. The olive tree metaphor explains that, because of this rejection, the natural, cultivated olive branches were cut off.

In the text, the Gentiles were represented as wild olive branches grafted onto the cultivated trunk. But, upon the return of Jesus, those branches that were cut off (Israel) will be grafted back onto the olive tree of the Lord. The gentile Church and Israel will stand side by side. On this point, I want to ask your opinion. What do you think the text says? What else could the Bible be declaring here?

One detail needs to be put here, at the end of this story. Over the ages, the Church hasn't been a friend of Israel! I grew up with many very close Jewish friends, and I personally know their plight cannot be envied. Their pain is real! Since the end of the nineteenth century, the Church's attitude toward Israel has been changing. More and more, the Church recognizes God's call to the Jewish people.

A word to every Jew reading this: I realize that this was probably hard to read. Do your research to see if it stands up to serious examination. **But, most of all, please forgive the Church for all the evil she has done to you!**

You may have noted the absence of the Muslim world in this discussion. I sincerely regret not being able to develop more on these pages. There are numerous biblical declarations concerning the Muslim people. The prophetic picture is much like the evening news on different television channels. Some of the reports are very bad, while others are very good. **The Bible does paint a fantastic picture of the reconciliation of Jews, Gentiles, and Muslims.** We must come to the point of forgiving one another. Jesus makes that possible!

Perhaps you are Asian or have a connection and want to know how Asian countries play in to the Biblical prophecies of Armageddon. The Asian world has had virtually no impact on Israel over the centuries. **Asia and Israel are not neighbors** and their paths never crossed—until the twentieth century. That relationship changed because of the search for profit. Business interests have lead far-eastern countries to develop markets in and around Israel. Is there a connection between our Asian countries and the "Kings of the East" spoken about in Revelation? We do not know; perhaps, but this has not happened yet.

Now it is time to take a look at why the unified church is an important sign to look for as we approach Armageddon—and a sure indicator that all things are not yet in place for the return of Jesus to fight the final battle.

CHAPTER 9

GOD WORKS IN THE UNIFIED CHURCH

THE CHURCH WILL BE POWERFUL.

> "And it shall come to pass in the last days, says God, that I will pour out of My Spirit on all flesh; your sons and your daughters shall prophesy, your young men shall see visions, your old men shall dream dreams. And on My menservants and on My maids I will pour out My Spirit in those days; and they shall prophesy."
>
> —Acts 2:17-18

Peter gave a powerful message that day. He quoted from the Old Testament book of Joel. The verses following this quote reiterate signs of the last times on earth. Let us concentrate on verses 17 and 18. My heart beats faster every time I read this two-thousand-year-old prophecy about four things God will do:

1. THE CHURCH WILL BE PROPHETIC.

God proposed this from the beginning, but the Church dropped the ball. What does this mean? Here, the word **prophetic** means that the Church will *edify, exhort, and comfort men* (1 Corinthians 14:3). Prophetically, the Church should never be out to pick a fight, or criticize, or curse fellow men. This book aims to share biblical truth to see **you** encouraged in this time of trial. The Bible's message is a buoy of hope in an ocean of despair.

Multitudes will be prophesying in one manner or another. They will be from different social statuses. Imagine all the various subcategories: diverse races, different economic levels, and varied educational levels. The old are present with the young. Women are there right beside the men! Enough said? The Church will be powerful only when all believers come on board. Then, there will only be one class—Unity First Class for all.

What will powerful Christians look like? Will they be protesting and rioting in the streets? Of course not! Burning down buildings and turning cars over? I think not. Will they be making demands on the government? Not at all! Will they stop traffic? No, for sure!

They will be in the streets singing praise to the

Lord. You will hear Christian music on the radio waves. They will be praying for the healing of the sick as Jesus commanded them to do in Mark 16:17-18. The same verses declare that demons will flee at the name of Jesus. All of this is clearly written in the Bible. You will see all this with your own eyes. **The Church will go public with all this!**

Christians will be going about doing good in every conceivable way. Something good may even happen to you. They will be doing random acts of kindness and love, freely given—with no self-interest! Tremendous power will be released when Christians rediscover generous living and giving. Humbly, I can say that I have started to taste this, and it is terrific!

Christianity has a horrible reputation when believers try to force their faith on people. When life, love, healing, and freedom from demons are offered to the masses, there will be different reaction.

All this will not stop the world from hating Christians. It has been mentioned already, but I want to make sure you understand that this is coming! Are you in, or are you out?

2. THE CHURCH WILL BE PURE AND MATURE.

> *Husbands, love your wives, just as Christ also loved the church and gave Himself for*

> *her, that He might sanctify and cleanse her with the washing of water by the word, that He might present her to Himself a glorious church, not having spot or wrinkle or any such thing, but that she should be holy and without blemish.*
>
> —Ephesians 5:25-27

I remember my wedding day and the first moment I saw my bride. She came down the aisle on her father's arm. What a beauty! To me, she seemed to be utterly without blemish. The human institution of marriage is in sync with what the Bible calls the Church's marriage to Jesus Christ. The Church is the Bride, and Jesus is the Groom. The image speaks of this spiritual couple that lives in a harmonious relationship. Jesus takes care of his Bride, and he purifies her in ways that words have a hard time communicating.

The result is that the Bride does not have a *spot or wrinkle or any such thing. She will be holy and without blemish.* Jesus sees her as beautiful. However, we haven't seen or fully imagined that yet. Still, the Bible promises that the Church will be **holy** and **beautiful**. Please notice, it is Jesus that brings the Church into holiness. Jesus transforms individual lives. His current project also includes the transformation of his Church.

Please do not let this become a pothole for you. Some resist Christianity because they do not want what they think is a dull and restrictive lifestyle. Let's talk about what **being holy is *not***: Holiness does *not* mean strict observance of ceremonial or dietary rules. It is *not* a state of enlightenment, *not* becoming a begging monk living on the streets, *not* living a restrictive lifestyle, nor being a hermit. Biblically, there isn't anything we can do to *earn* holiness. Being holy is simply allowing God to change our hearts. The resulting change in lifestyle should be evident—and I promise you, never dull.

3. THE CHURCH WILL FUNCTION AS GOD INTENDED!

And He Himself [Jesus] gave some to be apostles, some prophets, some evangelists, and some pastors and teachers, for the equipping of the saints for the work of ministry, for the edifying of the body of Christ, till we all come to the unity of the faith and of the knowledge of the Son of God, to a perfect man, to the measure of the stature of the fullness of Christ; that we should no longer be children, tossed to and fro and carried about with every wind of doctrine, by the trickery of men, in the cunning craftiness of deceitful plotting, but, speaking the truth in love, may grow up in all things into Him who is the head—Christ—from whom the whole body, joined and knit together by what every joint supplies, according to the effective working by which every part does its share, causes growth of the body for the edifying of itself in love.

—Ephesians 4:11-16

The Church has been such a mixed bag. Some of the most important innovations have come from Christians within the Church. Books were a Christian invention. Codex, a primitive bound book, helped Christians better read the Bible. Scrolls were hard to carry around!

Over the centuries, the Church established specific core values in western cultures. The importance and value of the individual were emphasized. The notion of work ethic, honesty, and faithfulness have always played a central role in Church values.

Harvard and Yale were initially Bible training centers. Many other universities started in the same manner. Christian hospitals sprouted across the world as part of the Church's mission support.[18]

Those achievements are exemplary. But, the failures of the Church are all too obvious. In the end, the future of the Church will look like what Paul wrote to the Ephesians. Five specific ministries will be present in the Church: apostles, prophets, evangelists, pastors, and teachers. These ministries will function **until the Church**

"grows up in all things into Him who is the head—Christ—." We have a long way to go until we get there, don't we?

These ministries can be present in churches but carrying different names. Each of these five ministries has specific **functions** in the Church. It isn't possible to explain all that here. The names of the ministries were not intended to be **titles**. In some ways, Church ministry can be compared to political service. Whenever those in authority stray away from the notion of loving service to the people, abuses will become evident. To complete this description, service to the people is meant to accompany devotion to God.

The people serving in these ministries are not superheroes! They are men and women just like you and me. But, they have been called to a particular task. Collectively they are called to help the Church mature.

Are you familiar with the parable of the Sower from Matthew 13? If not, here is a quick reminder. Jesus told of a farmer who scattered his precious seeds, but some fell in rocks with little soil, some fell in the open where birds could snatch them up, some fell among thorns that grew up to choke them out, and some fell on good soil. Read for yourself what happened! Israel was an agricultural society. Jesus was speaking the language of the large crowd that had gathered to hear him teach. He said that the seed was the Word of God planted in the earth to grow and grow to maturity. At harvest time, Jesus will say, *gather the wheat into my barn* (Matthew 13:30). That original grain reproduced itself and has grown into maturity.

The basic storyline of Matthew 13 is this—both good and evil will grow to **maturity** together. Yes, side by side! There will be one harvest, and you can imagine the rest. Where are you in this story?

You probably broke a shock absorber or two in those potholes. I challenge you to find a Bible on the shelf or on line and read for yourself what is written. Does the Bible say all that I have shared with you? If it does, isn't it possible that these sayings are true? If these sayings *are* correct, what are the consequences for you and me?

4. GOD WILL POUR OUT HIS SPIRIT

> *"And it shall come to pass afterward Tha t I will pour out My Spirit on all flesh; Your sons and your daughters shall prophesy, Your old men shall dream dreams, Your young men shall see visions."*
>
> —Joel 2:28

He is going to do it! The whole world will be aware that something unusual and God-like is going on. People will encounter the Lord's presence through daily events and directly by the manifestation of his Spirit. These verses are promises for us all. But not all will get on this train. Numerous so-called believers will even jump off the train.

You will be able to clearly see the difference between the work of God and the work of Satan. I painted that statement with a very wide brush.

> *"Then you shall again discern between the righteous and the wicked, between one who serves God and one who does not serve Him."*
>
> —Malachi 3:18

You may be struggling with some of these potholes. Do yourself a favor. Don't systematically reject what could be causing you problems. All of this is really in the Bible. Think about what is troubling you, and then pray about it. You may say, "Pray? Who, me?" Yes, you. Try this prayer:

"I don't understand some things, and I don't know if I even want to understand. God, I ask you to show me if this is true. If it is, what should I do? In Jesus' name. Amen."

I didn't expect to write that, and you didn't expect to read it. But, there it is, and I'll leave it. *Seek, and you will find.*

PART III

—

AFTER ARMAGEDDON

—

So, what *does* the Bible say about what happens after Jesus' return? In other words, what happens after Armageddon? Throughout the Bible, there are explanations of what will happen:

> *For behold, I create new heavens and a new earth; and the former shall not be remembered or come to mind.*
>
> —Isaiah 65:17

> *Nevertheless we, according to His prom-*

ise, look for new heavens and a new earth in which righteousness dwells.

—2 Peter 3:13

These are not isolated verses. What do these verses seem to say to you? Can we work on a general agreement here? Either the world goes up in a puff of smoke, or the world is recreated. Sincerely, you can forget the puff of smoke. The transformed world is going to keep on going. Nor was Jesus speaking of the astrological "Age of Aquarius" as some have wondered; Bible scholars all agree. But what about this "new earth"?

How can the world be totally recreated? Let's consider the character of God. God is the ultimate "superpower." A more technical description of God can be found in the word **omnipotent**, which means having limitless ability and power.

God can do anything he so chooses to do. In the rationalist mindset, this type of power does not exist. Omnipotence doesn't seem to be a valid notion anymore. This comes from our limited mental capacity to comprehend such power. Can you grasp the power to create and then recreate the world? I seriously doubt anyone has the mental capacity to do so but, don't take that personally. If God is omnipotent, he has no difficulty in such areas. If God has to align with our mental prowess to understand his moving, he has a severe handicap, doesn't he? That was a bump in the road. So where are you now on the road to Armageddon? Is your heart still quaking as the Doomsday Clock continues to *TICK-TICK-TICK*? Where does your hope lie?

CHAPTER 10

FACING ARMAGEDDON

We have arrived! We have faced Armageddon as simply as we could. We have taken as direct a journey as we could to see what the world sees, hear what the Bible says, understand how the Church fits in, and decide where you are on this road trip. If you made it this far, you have avoided many potholes!

All along the way I have promised you that if you keep reading I will give you reason to hope and not fear. At last we are here! Now is the time to answer the big question. "How do I conquer my doomsday fears?"

First, you have to know where your hope lies right now.

NO HOPE!

> *Therefore remember that you, once Gentiles in the flesh, …that at that time you*

were without Christ…having no hope and without God in the world.

—Ephesians 2:11-12

The world is depressed. The little, old invisible coronavirus has stripped away many of our illusions and dreams. The masses confined because of the coronavirus have been very uncomfortable gazing at themselves in the mirror, alone and suddenly helpless. The lack of a genuine inner life has come to the surface. If this is you, then you may have picked up this book because you are tired of being that person described in Ephesians as "having no hope and without God in the world." Let me help you up out of that pothole.

Have you asked yourself, "Where are we going? Where is this leading us? Is this all there is?"

First, you are not alone. There are generations alive today that are without an anchor. There is no longer a fixed point in people's lives—that singular place or person that doesn't move. Perhaps you, like many others, are tossed to and fro by the waves of the six o'clock news.

If there be a God, this surely would be an excellent common ground to meet him. Airports in many countries have a giant bullseye on the floor in the main area of the terminal. A sign overhead indicates this is a meeting point—a safe place to find or be found. That spot provides security for all those that are, or have been, or will be—**lost**. God is waiting there for you.

Do you know what is worse than having no hope? Having false hope—hope in something or someone that is not what they claim to be. Someone with no hope is more inclined to accept true hope in Christ than someone with false hope. Those that wallow in false hope are seldom aware of it. They are in grave danger!

FALSE HOPE!

The Old Testament speaks of ancient people who placed their hope in wooden idols that neither speak nor hear. This happens all the time today, but people often do not realize it. Perhaps you have put your trust in something or someone that will not hold up in the end, only you do not realize it. Forgive me, this section may be hard to accept—a pothole. Please don't skip around it, though. Be open.

Let me be honest. For a while, in my 20s, I was deeply involved in New Age. My initiation came through psychedelic drugs, and that lead directly into paranormal experiences. Reincarnation, channeling, trances, and astrology were my daily bread. I did some strange things, dabbling in the occult, astrology, and mysticism. I actually prayed to idols. I even got upset with them, but they never answered me. No tree or plank or beam will ever answer. The wood, cement, and plastic idols that fill the shelves in home decoration stores won't do any better.

Here is my personal definition of an idol: 1) that which is most important in your life; 2) the object of your obsession or your dependency. Modern-day idols take on specific forms:

SECULAR IDOLS

Cultural – A cultural idol is something that we need for security, or comfort, or pleasure. It takes on primary importance in one's life. Craving that **buzz** from the music, film, video games, virtual reality headsets, television series, the telephone, and the web have deformed our priorities. Cultural idols can take on an addictive characteristic. Do you have a cultural idol?

Economic – People invest their lives, their very souls, in the hope of financial success, often demonstrated through material possession. How many people orbit about a singular notion, "How can I make it"? Many are thrown on human junk heaps when that dream seems unattainable.

King David, of Old Testament fame, addressed this issue in military language:

> *Some trust in chariots, and some in horses; but we will remember the name of the Lord our God. They have bowed down*

and fallen; but we have risen and stand upright.

—Psalms 20:7-8

Technological - You gotta be hip, right? The latest device is undoubtedly the avenue to feel good and to impress all at the same time. Mobile phone envy created by communications companies is astounding. "Your phone really isn't you. You need our phone to be you. Don't you see?"

Sexual – As I have already mentioned, I had a hippie passport. In my 20s, I was of that nation. I left that country long ago when I entered Jesus' kingdom. In my former life, I was drug-dependent and sex-dependent. I'm being honest and hope that isn't too hard to swallow. When I compare the two dependencies, I know that sex-dependency had a stronger hold on my life than drugs. I was instantly delivered of that, and my 47-year marriage stands as a monument to that victory. Sex is promoted everywhere, a false hope based on personal satisfaction. Pleasure-seeking is an oppressive master.

I'm being very bold with you—Jesus can deliver you from that dependency, that idol. You may need this **right now**!

RELIGIOUS IDOLS

Usually, people imagine idols in a religious context. That may be the case, but *the times, they are a-changin'* (thanks, Bob Dylan). Today, the secular has taken the place of the sacred. That is why I listed secular (non-religious) idols first. But, many of us truly do idolize our religion, or our religious practices, over our relationship with God himself.

Remember, an idol is that which is most important in your life. The object of your obsession or your dependency. Consider these:

Religious objects - Do you have an altar in your house? Do you pray to pieces that you believe send your prayers to your ancestors, to a saint, to any number of gods, or to God himself? If that is your case, I would like to say to you, with all the kindness I can muster in my heart, you have placed your hope in inanimate objects and not God himself.

Religious people - Some of us have fallen into the trap of idolizing a person, a human being, trusting in that person to be our protector, our rescuer. If this is you, don't be too hard on yourself. People can be very persuasive, and some charlatans are working very hard to deceive you. This person could be a religious or political figure, a social leader, a celebrity, or a person close to your heart.

You might idolize a person who has passed away but who you turn to for guidance or protection, such as a saint, or an ancestor. You might place all your trust in the person you see in the mirror! No human being can stand in the place of God. Any human being will eventually fail you.

Religious doctrine - There is another stealthier idol: religious doctrine. People hold to specific dogmas, or beliefs, and they are convinced that just by having these beliefs they are secure—everything is good. Solid beliefs are a sound foundation for life. But, when those beliefs don't translate into everyday reality, when they don't line up with a personal relationship with God himself, the train runs off the track.

For example, do you believe that your baptism, your confirmation, your doctrines, your religious gestures, or your parents' faith will protect you in a time of need? These things are good, but they are only outward religious gestures. They must align with genuine devotion to God. Yes, these things have become idols for many people.

Have you decided where your hope lies yet? Do you have no hope at all in this world and where we are headed? Or do you fear your hope may be false hope, placed in people, things, or beliefs that won't hold up? Let me encourage you. Hope lies just ahead!

TRUE HOPE!

What is hope, really? Is it a child's fantasy? A pipe dream? Foolishness? Or is hope something tangible and real? Rodney Buchanan held theological degrees from Asbury College and Ashland Theological Seminary. He pastored in the Methodist Church for forty-two years. He authored numerous works that centered on the theme of Christian hope. He really got it right when he said:

"To hope is to give up control and give the control to God. It replaces confidence in ourselves with confidence in God. It is not wishing, for wishing keeps things within the bounds of our own imaginations. Hope is open-ended—an expectation that God will do something greater than we could have ever dreamed. Wishing is fantasy, hope is based in a grand reality—the person and character of a loving, ever-imaginative God who always has our best in mind." [19]

Dr. Buchanan went on to emphasize how God infuses hope in us by quoting the apostle Paul:

For all the promises of God in Him are Yes, and in Him Amen, to the glory of God through us. Now He who establishes us with you in Christ and has anointed us is God, who also has sealed us and given us the Spirit in our hearts as a guarantee.
—2 Corinthians 1:20-22

The biblical God is a creator, provider, protector, judge, healer, peace giver, guide, ever-present, everlasting, master, and the all-encompassing LORD!

Yes, it's true! You can be free from any fear of the end of the world by placing your hope, your trust and faith in the One who created it all, who is in complete control, and who loves you, knows you, and accepts you where you are, right now.

Real hope is based on the love of God for man. He cares for me, and he cares for you. Remember, the cosmos doesn't love you or even know your name. I would like to share a few verses with you that underline that hope which is found in one place: Jesus Christ:

> *For God so loved the world that He gave His only begotten Son, that whoever believes in Him should not perish but have everlasting life.*
>
> —John 3:16

> *To them God willed to make known what are the riches of the glory of this mystery among the Gentiles: which is Christ in you, the hope of glory.*
>
> —Colossians 1:27

> *For I know the thoughts that I think toward you, says the Lord, thoughts of peace*

and not of evil, to give you a future and a hope.

—Jeremiah 29:11

Now may the God of hope fill you with all joy and peace in believing, that you may abound in hope by the power of the Holy Spirit.

—Romans 15:13

For the grace of God that brings salvation has appeared to all men, teaching us that…we should live soberly, righteously, and godly in the present age, looking for the blessed hope and glorious appearing of our great God and Savior Jesus Christ…

—Titus 2:11-13

These verses are for us in this life, in this world, and even during and after Armageddon. The Holy Scriptures abundantly declare that God gives us hope in every situation. Whether you are in the depths of personal collapse or the final passage to the other side, he is there. There is hope in this life and the next.

I'm not crazy enough to want all the calamities described in this book about Armageddon to fall on me. But, if they do come, I am sure of two things:

1. I will not forsake God during times of trouble.
2. He will not forsake me.

Please try to shut everything out right now. Enter a no-noise zone! You are invited to consider all that you have read. Right now, I'm inserting a prayer that you can say in your own words.

"It seems awkward to say 'Heavenly Father,' but I need hope in my life, and I come to you as my source.

I need to know that you forgive me for all the wrong I've done.

I believe Jesus did die for my sins on the cross.

I ask you to deliver me from my life of ego, vanity, and despair.

I need to trust in someone, and you seem worthy.

I give you control of my life; please guide me.

This all seems too much to ask, but my heart cries out for you.

Please come to me and live in me.

I ask this in the name of Jesus. AMEN!"

And that is the answer, my friend! That is how you can conquer your fear of doomsday, and while you are at it, be free of any fear of death or calamity on this earth.

THE OTHER SIDE OF HOPE

Did you just pray that prayer from your heart? If so, you are forever able to enjoy the peace of having true hope. No one can ever take that away from you! I'd like to leave three last points with you:

1. While we are waiting on Armageddon, we have a lotta livin' to do. The road before you has many more potholes than you found in this book. But, the Lord will lead you to your final destination, in heaven, or on this earth.
2. Ask God to direct you to other believers who can accompany you on this pilgrimage. He will do it.
3. I believe the Lord can cause these following verses to bubble up from your spirit. Your life will change if you prayed the above prayer and meant it.

PSALM 23: THE SHEPHERD'S PSALM

The Lord is my shepherd; I shall not want.

He makes me to lie down in green pastures; He leads me beside the still waters.

He restores my soul; He leads me in the paths of righteousness for His name's sake.

Yea, though I walk through the valley of the shadow of death, I will fear no evil; for You are with me; Your rod and Your staff, they comfort me.

You prepare a table before me in the presence of my enemies; You anoint my head with oil; my cup runs over.

Surely goodness and mercy shall follow me all the days of my life; and I will dwell in the house of the Lord forever.

ABOUT THE AUTHOR

John Tressel, originally from Canton, Ohio, is the president of the Institute of Theology by Extension (INSTE) Bible College in France. INSTE courses help men and women become disciples of Jesus Christ and provide training for those entering the ministry.

INSTE is an educational organization established in forty countries, teaching in at least sixteen languages. John is responsible for all French-speaking countries, ten of which have schools already established. He also serves on the national leadership team for ANTIOCHE, or Antioch Network of Churches, a church-planting organization established in eight countries as of 2021.

John was a founding partner of Editions MENOR, a French publisher serving the entire French-speaking world. MENOR has published over one hundred books, primarily in the field of Christian Church life.

John taught in numerous Bible schools on four continents. Ministry has led him to fifteen countries throughout the world. He has published two books in French, primarily focused on the Church and prophecy.

John and his wife, Gloria, have been missionaries in France for over forty-five years through French World Ministries. They have served as church planters, pastors, teachers, and traveling ministers focused on helping revive struggling churches and launch new ministries. John and Gloria have given themselves to the French-speaking world, including the many Muslims living in France. They currently live in Alsace, France. Their three children were raised in France—literally in the four corners of the country.

Contact John: endoftheworld@gmx.com

UPCOMING BOOKS:

John has two books scheduled for release in 2023. The first covers the important topic of welcoming, encouraging, and correcting the prophetic gifts in the local church. The second discusses in laymen's terms the biblical role of the church as we approach the rapture and tribulation period.

Subscribe to Encourage Publishing on line to be notified about John's upcoming titles.

https://www.encouragepublishing.com

ENDNOTES

[1] https://tinyurl.com/wardeathdata
[2] https://www.prio.org/publications/11181
[3] https://tinyurl.com/doomsday2020
[4] https://thebulletin.org/doomsday-clock/
[5] https://tinyurl.com/Ukrainesunflower
[6] https://tinyurl.com/UNfamine
[7] https://tinyurl.com/PCMatthew24
[8] https://www.biblestudytools.com/lexicons/greek/kjv/aion.html - The Greek word for "age" in this passage is defined in Strong's Concordance, referenced in the word key G165
[9] https://biblehub.com/greek/3061.htm
[10] https://tinyurl.com/quakesurge
[11] https://tinyurl.com/2010volcano
[12] https://tinyurl.com/MacArthurfarewell
[13] https://tinyurl.com/Christianpopdata
Data from Todd M. Johnson and Brian J. Grim, eds. World Religion Database (Leiden/Boston: Brill, 2022).
[14] https://tinyurl.com/Ochab2020
[15] https://tinyurl.com/unreachedpeoples
[16] https://tinyurl.com/deserttofarm
[17] https://tinyurl.com/Jerusalempop
[18] https://uh.edu/engines/epi991.htm
[19] https://tinyurl.com/Buchanansermon

FULL CITES

[i] https://ourworldindata.org/war-and-peace
[ii] https://www.prio.org/publications/11181
[iii] https://thebulletin.org/doomsday-clock/2020-doomsday-clock-statement/
[iv] https://thebulletin.org/doomsday-clock/
[v] www.bloomberg.com/news/articles/2022-04-01/ukraine-sunflower-oil-shortage-hits-food-from-chips-to-cookies
[vi] news.un.org/en/story/2020/09/1072712
[vii] https://biblehub.com/commentaries/pulpit/matthew/24.htm
[viii] https://greeklexicon.org/lexicon/strongs/165/
[ix] https://biblehub.com/greek/3061.htm
[x] www.nbcnews.com/science/science-news/worldwide-surge-great-earthquakes-seen-past-10-years-n233661
[xi] www.theguardian.com/world/2014/aug/24/iceland-volcano-uk-airspace-civil-aviation-authority
[xii] www.americanrhetoric.com/speeches/douglasmacarthur-farewelladdress.htm
[xiii] https://en.wikipedia.org/wiki/List_of_Christian_denominations_by_number_of_members#Christianity_%E2%80%93_2.6_billion
[xiv] www.forbes.com/sites/ewelinaochab/2020/02/18/persecuted-christians-are-not-given-much-hope-in-2020/?sh=295dcd126889
[xv] www.pioneerseurope.org/en/Stories/Unreached-Peoples
[xvi] www.csmonitor.com/1987/0519/dsand.html

[xvii] worldpopulationreview.com/world-cities/jerusalem-population

[xviii] https://uh.edu/engines/epi991.htm

[xix] www.sermoncentral.com/sermons/there-is-hope-rodney-buchanan-sermon-on-christmas-advent-74457?page=3&wc=80)

www.ingramcontent.com/pod-product-compliance
Lightning Source LLC
Chambersburg PA
CBHW071856070526
44583CB00016B/1715